Good Grief

The Highs and Lows of Healing

Isabella Tesnow

Made with ❤ on the BookLeaf Publishing Platform
www.bookleafpub.in
www.bookleafpub.com

Dedication

To Dad:

You have unfillable shoes, I can only hope to do half the things you did in your short time on Earth. In that case, I hope this book sells more than *Plateau Surfers* ever did (Ha-ha!). I miss you more than these words could ever portray, and I love you more than I could ever say.

Preface

Good Grief is a journal of sorts, a collection of my struggles with mental health, finding my identity, and losing someone important to me. Written in the spirit of honesty and vulnerability, this collection is a reminder that growth and healing are more demanding than what meets the eye. In an attempt to find hope within despair, this book is for those who have kept their heart locked away for so long, who hold in all their pain. These poems are some of the keys that will one day free my heart. I hope it inspires you to get a keychain.

Acknowledgements

Thank you to my lovely friends and family who have encouraged me to believe in myself and my work. Without your support, I would not have gotten here this quickly. Thank you to my lovely professors, teachers, and guides who have reignited my passion for learning and creating. And thank you, readers, for taking the time to get a peek inside my mind.

1. silence

the sound of silence

was never familiar

for when it was quiet

it was the loudest

static and anxiety

never feeling in the clear

with quiet came thunder

calm before the storm

anticipation filling the air

never sure when to expect

the next boom

2. what you don't know

don't worry
I will sing to you
and rub your back
as you close your eyes
and head to sleep
no need to be scared
I know
you don't understand
neither do I
no need to cry
shh shh
don't want them
to hear you
you are safe
I will protect you
with my life
until you start snoring

then I will leave your side
tip toe past the mess
hoping to not be caught
in the crossfire
if I am lucky
I will make it to safety

lay my head down
and wait for the dust
to finally settle
so I can drain my eyes
of the welled up waters
then I will join you
in slumber
and hope for dreams
instead of nightmares

3. uncertainty

is there a way
to stop this madness?
the hurt
the violence
the sadness?
swear I'm trying
but nothing happens

continuing cycles
that end in tragedy
swore that this would never
happen to me
but it is,
so now,
what do I do?
drop what I've got
and turn to you?

I can't
your're not even there
and if you were
I'm not sure you'd care
I'm not sure of anything
except I know nothing

and that the pain from this life
is crushing

maybe one day I'll wake up
and not feel like back when
until then,
I'll just write with my pen
and maybe someday
it will all make sense

4. the cycle

...caught in a loop
trapped in insanity
spinning in circles
what happened to gravity?
demons of my mind
win every time
losing grip on reality
what does it take,
death and destruction
to rid of dysfunction?

caught in a loop
trapped in insanity
veered off path
by stress and calamity
trapped in a world
with no amenity
where is the love?
did it leave?
pain in my chest
can hardly breathe

caught in a loop
trapped in insanity

seemingly lost
searching for humanity
will this pain
affect my longevity?
where is my soul?
I feel so numb
tell me when
this cycle is done...

5. proceed with caution

the salty taste lingers on your face

eyes red as the blood that flows through your veins

can barely breathe

heart clenched in agony

lungs feel as if you're drowning

the darkness courses through your body

you are itching to do it again

even though you understand it's wrong

the external pain helps soften the internal

(or so you think)

but you're falling down a deep, dark hole

and one day

you will hit the ground.

6. sense of self

like sand on the beach

I pick you up
thousands of grains
held in my hands

suddenly lose hold of you

slipping slowly
through my fingers

expediting the process
as I struggle to pile
pieces together again

but it's far too late

every time
I pick you up
you're never the same

7. love

I will hold my own hand

as I pick myself back up

after I've fallen for tricks

once again

led astray by my foolish hope

that loving others

can help them

reach for the better

but what good am I

I don't even try

to stop myself

from offering something

I've rarely been offered

rarely been given

rarely accepted

something I've never

given myself

didn't want to be selfish

thought I had to

give it away

that it was my job

to love

love

love

and never be heard

to never be truly loved

in return

8. how-to

wise beyond her years

so mature

so witty

so intelligent

and

so
so
so

beautiful

if you tell her

enough times

perhaps she won't see

behind the curtain

that veils

your sinister mind

previous voices doom her

say she is worthless

the chance to strike
—I mean—
save her

will fall into your lap

all you must do

is tell her everything

she wanted to hear

after that

she will

love
love
love you

until of her

there is nothing left

9. the trap

never quite realized
what attracted me to the spiral

the sinking feeling in the gut

but then I remember
how I first walked into a trap

was no ordinary knot

nor snare or snap

no, this trap

was so sophisticated
cultivated

over years

compounding
with every turn of the sun

was no trap of the body

but a trap of the mind

one that caught me

to keep me in line

told there was no way out

that I am stuck forever

and out of the cage

it is not much better

carried the trap

with me everywhere

never too worried

about its weight

staggering my walk
shattering my soul

convinced

this is how it's supposed to be

that I didn't deserve to know

what it meant to be free

10. pain

letting yourself feel again

after once so numb

body once served as protector

suddenly is safe

safe to let the tears
leak from my face

everything felt, all at once

a single sting
reminiscent of the others

finally smothered by crushing weight

that was there all along

but was I really so strong?

put it all to the side

to abide by the rules

in the game of life

now that I've made it
to this other side

the grass isn't green

but there is water

locked behind dams
long abandoned by their operator

how do you let

the river flood

so that the trees

can be reminded

that they were thirsty?

do I release it all
and let it consume me?

or do I let it leak
until it can be set free?

is there a right
or a wrong way?

the answer could soon

be clear as day

but even then, sometimes

the sky is grey.

11. just a bitch

anger masks my melancholy

the firey blaze hides the truth

maybe if they think I'm a bitch

they'll never ask what's wrong

assume that I'm like this

so I don't have to choke on my tears

the scrunch of my brow

is because I am mean

it has nothing to do

with everything underneath

I'm quiet with rage

so be sure to tip-toe around me

and I'll be sure

to bring the eggshells

so you have something to walk on

don't have to worry about me

watch the steam

blow from my ears

just don't ask me

what my problem is

because then

I may prove you right

12. the little girl in the mirror

sometimes

when I dare to look into my own eyes

I catch a glimpse of her

the little girl in the mirror

never afraid to smile with her teeth
no problem being caught drawing at midnight
and ran as if the wind carried her

never worried about what others may think

felt intensely, without fear

& never scared to love others, or herself

the longer I search for her
the more I hear her shout our name

reminding me of who I am, not what I was

kept hidden in the depths of my soul
she slowly finds her way back to me

and I to her

for that little girl
lives within me
is me

and she never left

13. I have a question

how do you celebrate the death of someone you were
never ready to lose?

the remnants of a person loved, left the living battered
and bruised

many of which fear death too much, or not enough

smoking, drinking, drugging the pain away

dancing with death with every inhale, sip and swallow

caught in the wonder of what could have, should have,
would have been

the remaining questions left forever unanswered

14. are you there?

sometimes I feel
like I am talking to air
hoping that the wind
sweeps these sounds
in your direction

do you hear me?
or do my cries
fall upon empty skies
and disappear as quickly
as you did?

15. still wondering

could really use some help here

maybe if I beg a thousand times

you'll suddenly appear

like a voice in my head

booming with glorious advice

and post-humous guidance

if I think hard enough

surely you can suddenly pop up

and answer my thousand questions

is it really so hard

for someone with no ties

to this material world

to stop by every once and a while

and remind me

that I'm not alone?

16. pep talk

no more breakdowns
it's time to break through

change is coming
do you feel it too?

the world's getting hotter
but why would they bother?

they just want to use you
for your spirit, your soul, your love

the force is inside you
stop searching above

darkness in the world
keeps dimming your light

but did you ever think
you could be so bright?

stop flipping the switch
go ahead and remove it

your yearning, ambition
that's where the truth sits.

17. confidence

been fighting daily with myself
causing issues of mental health

but maybe today I'll see things a new way
keep on this path, no going astray

can't be hard
gotta dive head-first

think I'm ready now
so give me your worst

constantly growing
now that its showing

it's mine for the taking
don't be mistaken

waited too long,
but better late than never

going after what's mine
yeah, I'm a go-getter

ask where I'll be in five
and I'll say
"better"

better than before
it's for sure

confidence not lacking
the tools I need, I'm packing

so send it all my way world
I'm ready
feet on the ground
with my head in the clouds
and still keeping it steady

18. the ultimate gift

waves
crashing and pulling

salty air
refreshing

sun
beaming bright

clouds
painting the sky

a gift
that cannot be wrapped

gratitude
unspeakable

how did the world
once feel so small?

the water rises
and falls

endless blue
stretches the horizon

a reminder

of how small
you are

and how big
you can become

19. personal reminders

take a moment, look up to the sky

watch the birds as they fly

listen to the drumming of the rain

watch someone chase the train

miss the heat of summer's day

wish for winter while it's away

sing your heart out to your favorite song

dance with your friends all night long

get lost in your art and creativity

hold back on grudge and negativity

so long to go, but look how far you've come

your work is far from over, far from done

so take that moment, take a breath

never know which may lead to death

and if that moment makes you cry

let that damn tear drop from your eye.

20. grow

no longer in hiding
sprouts begin to show
bringing to light
who you are, what you know

come to the surface
let your roots guide you
do not be afraid
reveal how you grew

take what you've learned
the unforgettable teachings
come forth and accept
the world's greetings

21. gone, not lost

everywhere I go, I find you

I hear you in the laughs, I hear you in the cries

I see you in the trees, I see you in the skies

I see you in everyone, your sisters and your brother

I hear you in your father's voice, see you in paintings by your mother

no matter where I go, from you I cannot hide

I feel you in my spirit, forever you are my guide